Under A Maui Sun

A CELEBRATION OF THE ISLAND OF MAUI

Written by Penny Pence Smith

ISLAND HERITAGE PUBLISHING
A Division of The Madden Corporation

UNDER A MAUI SUN ™

ISLAND HERITAGE PUBLISHING
A Division of The Madden Corporation
99-880 Iwaena Street
Aiea, Hawaii 96701
(808) 487-7299

Project Director, Dixon J. Smith
Designer and Photography Editor, Paul Turley

First Edition, Fifth Printing — 1998

ISBN 0-89610-400-1

TABLE OF CONTENTS

A space–eye view of Maui.

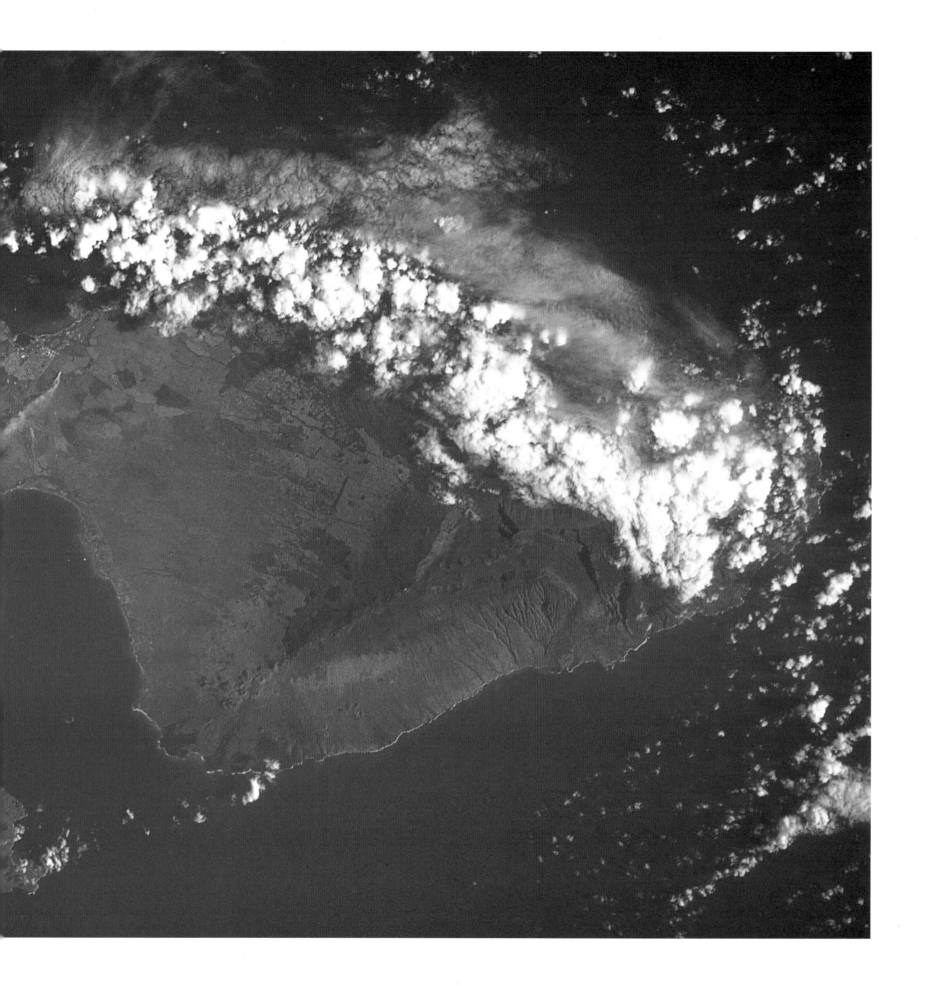

*IT IS NO SMALL WONDER THAT
THE ISLAND OF MAUI HAS BECOME THE MOST
DAZZLING JEWEL IN THE CROWN OF HAWAI'I*

Such stature is her natural inheritance for it was the magical demi-god Māui, whose name she bears, who snagged the sun to shine ever more brilliantly over her shores. Her Polynesian ancestors arrived about the time of King Arthur's Roundtable and their descendants today greet visitors from throughout the world with warmth, a pride born of long tradition, and great style. Maui has been called one of the most perfect paradises on earth – from her splendid shoreline, now an international watersports capital, to her exotic flowers exported world-wide, to her gifted and growing art community. Some metaphysicans call Maui the "Center of the Universe."

All such claims are her natural destiny.

"I come back to Maui again and again," says a visitor from America's Great Plains. "I can stand in these four square feet of beach and know that no matter how deep the snow is or how hard the freezing wind blows at home, or what the world conditions are elsewhere, the sun will be here – day after day. Somehow, some way I know I am destined to live under a Maui sun!"

This book is for those of us who have strolled Maui's beaches, relished her waterfalls and pools, her greenery and flowers. It is for all of us who know deep in our hearts that we, too, were intended to live life under her golden sun.

MISCHIEVOUS, MAGICAL MAUI - THE SUN AGREED TO SHINE MORE BRILLIANTLY HERE

Māui of the legends was a Hawaiian demi-god who flirted with fate and gained a reputation for his mischievousness and his magical creativity. According to the whims of its own birthright, today's Maui has become one of the most stylish and enchanting islands in the Hawaiian chain. From the tip of its highest and most obvious point, the rim of the Haleakalā crater, to its delicate secluded pools and waterfalls, Maui is where people of the world find peace, relaxation, inspiration – and whimsy!

Because the demigod Māui convinced the sun to shine specially over this island, sunsets are more magical than anyplace else on earth.

A spirit of lighthearted fun is in the air, in perfect harmony with the island's namesake, Magical, Mischievous Māui.

1

Children, flowers and sand – three essential elements of Hawai'i.

" energetic, laughing keikis "

On the hillsides, small rural schools are nestled against sloping fields of sugar cane and serve as backdrops for soccer and softball games between energetic, laughing *keikis* — children. They will one day study mathematics, physics and political science in nearby high schools and later at distant colleges, but today they spend their after-school hours learning the ancient ancestral hula dances and chants, lei-making and other crafts of their grandparents.

In Lahaina, freckled blonde *Haoles* (Caucasians) wait tables, sell sunny fashions and lead tour groups alongside long-time Mauians. In Hāna, proud, sturdy Polynesian faces reflect true Hawaiian bloodlines, as their owners greet guests and diners at the Hotel Hāna Maui.

The flower lei has always communicated special messages in Hawai'i – Happy Birthday, Congratulations, I love You, Welcome – Come Back Soon.

Keikis learn fair play on the soccer fields of Maui. 3

Maui's spectacular beauty is both natural and magical.

Brisk tradewinds and beautiful surf have made Maui an international windsurfing capital.

This harmony of bloodlines and cultures generates a warmth and energy born of ancient tradition, and is wrapped around a stylish and contemporary life. It is reflected everywhere, from the upscale shopping and resort complexes of Kā'anapali Beach and Kīhei/Wailea to the magic of the sparkling waterfalls and pools around Hāna, from the bold and aggressive surf at Ho'okipa to the country quiet of Kula. Indeed, the true essence of Maui exists on three levels: in legend, through ancient Polynesian history, and in the contemporary lifestyle. Maui was named – by the ancient Polynesians – for a god born to a human mother who, reacting to a great famine on earth, sent her babe to sea in a fragile seaweed boat. Adrift and alone, he was discovered by the gods of the swirling seas, who adopted the child and bestowed upon him their magical powers. But Māui was a mischievous child, fond of frolicking and tricks. When he was eight years old, his guardians grew weary of his antics and returned the boy to his mother.

Māui's powerful lessons and gifts remained with him – as did his penchant for mischief. For example, he is said to have created the Hawaiian island chain – Hawai'i, Maui, Moloka'i, O'ahu and Kaua'i – by fishing for and catching the demon One-Tooth, who held the Pacific islands together under the sea. With the demon successfully snagged on the line, Māui's brothers ignored Māui's admonitions to not look back, and did so exclaiming "Look what you've caught!" The spell – and the line – broke! Only One-Tooth's quick wits saved the Hawaiian islands from being flung far into the Pacific. But other islands, including Tahiti, did not escape such a fate, and today it is said that Māui "fished" Tahiti from the ocean floor.

The many faces of Maui include one which smiles radiantly on ranch life.

" sparkling waterfalls and pools "

5

" he captured Lā, the sun, who lived in Haleakalā crater "

Dramatic sunrises are a major attraction of Haleakalā

Māui is also held responsible for the island's golden sunny weather, for he captured *Lā*, the sun, who lived in Haleakalā crater and set out daily on a capricious streak of light across the universe. Legend tells us that Māui netted Lā with a fish net (another version says he lassoed him), tied him to a tree and commanded him to shine continually so that Māui's mother, a tapa cloth maker, could use the warming rays to dry her wares more quickly. After much negotiation, the sun compromised with the young demi-god and agreed to move more slowly across Maui's sky for half the year.

Such persistence and foresight understandably fed Māui's reputation – as a great wonder-worker, as well as a great trickster.

A crater resident, the Silversword, catches the the sun's glistening rays, making it easy to understand why Haleakalā is called the "House of the Sun."

" dazzling crescent of shoreline "

Maui's shoreline changes dramatically in the sunset.

Ko Mauitinihanga koe, ("You, Maui of a Thousand Tricks"), and *Mauitikitiki* (Great Wonder Worker) were names given the legendary god by the first Polynesians who arrived on the island, which they subsequently named for him, about 900 A.D. These intrepid voyagers were part of a second major immigration sailing from the Marquesas where they are thought to have settled originally about 1500 B.C. They arrived on Maui in the shadow of a fiery Haleakalā volcano, at Kahikinui which they then called *Hāmoa.* This dazzling crescent of shoreline, still called Hāmoa, lies along the Hāna Coast.

Maui's sparkling waterfalls and pools abound for adventurers.

Remote, serene Hāna has changed little over the years – thanks to the protection afforded by the 52-mile road that winds along the edge of the coastline.

Comprising 728.6 square miles, Maui is divided into two sections – the eastern-most and largest portion rising from the ocean floor 19,000 feet to sea level and then another 10,023 to the tip of Haleakalā. On this portion of the island today rests historic Hāna, Maui's verdantly glorious upcountry, the beaches of Mākena and Kīhei, the resorts at Wailea, and the international windsurfing capital near Pā'ia. On the western portion of the island are the historic town of Lahaina, the lush Īao Valley, and the lovely resorts of Kā'anapali and Kapalua. Geologists say that Maui was originally much larger than it is today, comprising six volcanic peaks and all the terrain that today constitutes Maui, Kaho'olawe and Moloka'i. Erosion and natural forces ultimately split the land masses into three separate islands.

In the shadow of a Maui sunset it is sometimes difficult to recognize the current era.

" verdantly glorious upcountry "

Maui visitors enjoy the many opportunities to learn windsurfing skills.

"*a truly spirited heritage*"

With a truly spirited heritage, the people of
Maui could not help but take a visible role in the
formation and growth of the Hawaiian Islands.
It was on Maui that the first interisland clash
among the chieftains took place about 1300
A.D., an event that was to become commonplace in history as rulers of one island sought to
capture the peoples and territory of the other
islands, until Kamehameha the Great defeated
all the island chiefs and united the population.

*The hula is learned as early and as readily by Maui
youth as reading, writing and arithmetic.*

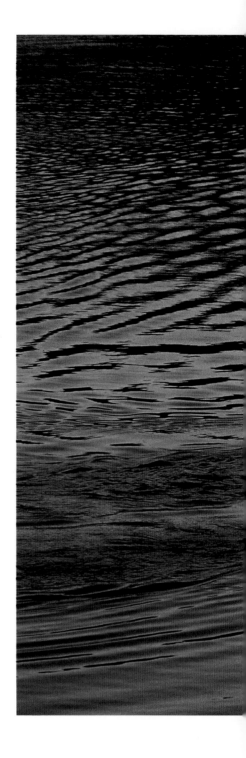

Maui paddlers stroke homeward into the setting sun.

" demise of ancient religious social taboos "

Maui's king Kahekili, said to be the true father of Kamehameha the Great, united his own people in 1776 by defeating the forces of Kalani'opu'u who ruled Hāna from Hawai'i, just across the channel.

Spiritual Maui also emanates from legend, and ancient origins. Hāna-born Ka'ahumanu, favorite wife of Kamehameha the Great, is credited with the demise of ancient religious social taboos. A spirited and powerful monarch, she dined publicly with a male relative, breaking the rule that forbade male and female Ali'i's to dine together, and thereby began unraveling other traditional mores.

Sometimes it is refreshing to fill the moment with a simple Maui view.

15

Tidepools reflected in the sunset provide a world of wonders to explore.

Religion plays an important role in the life of Mauians, even along the rustic road to Hāna.

Christian missionaries arriving around 1820 found a population essentially without religious structure or leadership. Ka'ahumanu personally resisted the teachings of Christianity until she was near death. Nonetheless, life on Maui changed significantly when these strangers from New England introduced their beliefs and teachings.

Spiritual seekers continue to search out Maui's peaceful atmosphere even today. The "flower children" of the 1970s quickly discovered Maui and many new age metaphysicians continue to call the island home. An order of monks based in the Maui hills, are commercial bee-keepers and sell honey products to the Mainland.

A pastoral way of life typifies Upcountry Maui.

The bursting beauty of Upcountry's protea flowers is a world-wide favorite among designers and florists.

Maui farmers and flower growers are also world-renowned. The exotic proteas and other floral delights of Upcountry make up the dramatic lobby arrangements in the island's hotels, and are sold world-wide as well as in the local grocery markets.

Maui came to the attention of the outside world in 1778 when Captain James Cook first saw it from Hāna Bay, but sailed on to the Big Island of Hawai'i without leaving the ship. In 1786, French Captain Jean Francois de Galaupe de la Perouse became the first European to formally land on Maui – not far from Mākena Beach at a site which today bears his name. Only five years later Captain George Vancouver gifted King Kamehameha with the island's first cattle. "Protected" by the monarch, the herd roamed wild on the island. Years later their offspring constituted the beginnings of a new cattle industry for Maui.

" exotic proteas and other floral delights "

Taro was a staple of the ancient Polynesians and is still cultivated today.

" capital of the Hawaiian kingdom "

The shoreline of Lahaina has been a trademark of Maui's spirited good times from the time of the whaling fleets.

While several primary industries forged Maui's economic future, none left so colorful a mark as the whalers. In 1819, the whaling ship _Balena_ arrived at Lahaina Bay from New Bedford, Connecticut, to find a most accommodating tropical base. With the population of migratory whales that passed through Hawai'i's waters, and Maui's intoxicating people and weather, Lahaina quickly became a second home to whalers from all over the world.

The town of Lahaina was named the capital of the Hawaiian kingdom – a position it enjoyed until the capital was moved to Honolulu following the ultimate demise of the whaling industry. By then agriculture had taken firm root on Maui.

Whale Shark shares Maui waters with cautious companions.

Each year the sugar cane fields are burned to prepare the soil for the next crop.

In 1828 two Chinese merchants founded the Hungtai Sugar Works, the island's first commercial sugar operation, setting the momentum for what was to become Maui's most persistent industry. Major sugar operations followed as entrepreneurs like Claus Spreckles, George Wilfong and others planted the slopes of Haleakalā and the slopes of the West Maui Mountains. They exported their product throughout the world. The first Chinese contract laborers arrived to work the fields in 1852, adding yet another thread to the intricate weave of Maui's ethnic personality.

" Maui's most persistent industry "

" a bold step in agriculture "

Pineapple fields are etched against the Maui hillsides.

Maui's Tedeschi Vineyards now produce the island's first fine champagnes and wines.

The sugar business also instigated the creation of two railway systems on the island – one between Lahaina and Kā'anapali and one between Pā'ia and Kahului – and encouraged the development of international steamship freight activity to and from the Kahului Harbor.

Pineapple, as a Maui crop, was first planted at Ha'ikū in 1890, introduced by missionary descendant Dwight Baldwin. Maui again took a bold step in agriculture as recently as 1984, when the local Tedeschi Winery introduced Maui's first home-grown champagne. Locally brewed lager beer is also commercially available.

Even though it is no longer part of the economic lifeblood of Hawai'i, the image of the pineapple is still synonymous with the islands.

25

A verdant pastiche creates a jigsaw puzzle from the volcano to the sea.

Sugar cane and pineapple account for only a small portion of the island's economy today, although it seems that to drive any distance on the island is to meander through an endless sea of these shimmering emerald fields. In truth, Maui's primary source of revenue is mostly derived from the visitors who explore those fields in rental cars – and from the development that has emerged in support of the visitor industry.

Still, the fields of cane and pineapple that remain – sloping gently up Haleakalā's foothills – are a reminder of the roots on which today's island economy was based.

Shops galore provide every imaginable type of gift for Lahaina visitors.

" an endless sea of these shimmering emerald fields "

" a 'paniolo' personality all its own "

Cattle ranching, part and parcel of Upcountry's personality, began in earnest on the slopes of Haleakalā in 1856 when ship captain James Makee imported cattle and turned his sugar plantation into grazing lands. Other plantation owners soon followed suit and Upcountry Maui has since been characterized by a "paniolo" personality all its own, still sought after by would-be ranchers who more often drive their four-wheel vehicles to the island beaches and bistros than their cattle to market!

An Upcountry lass sports a traditional paniolo hat.

transliteration modes in Hāna reflect the quiet charm of another era.

"Holistic Herding" on the ranchlands keeps the animals moving from one grazing spot to another in order to preserve the delicate cycle of vegetation.

Nothing's quite as colorful as a parade in Upcountry's Makawao.

The growth of agriculture and commerce, and the decline of the whaling industry, shifted Maui's political base from Lahaina to Wailuku, and nearby Kahului developed as the island's busiest commercial sea port. Maui, along with the other Hawaiian islands, became ever more visible and accessible following the overthrow of the Hawaiian monarchy and establishment of a territorial government in 1893, the annexation by the U.S. in 1898, and finally the granting of statehood in 1959. Today, Maui is the second largest in population of the islands, second largest as well in the number of visitors it attracts each year.

" the decline of the whaling industry
shifted Maui's political base from Lahaina to Wailuku "

Maui's agriculture thrives in tropical sun and rain.

Those visitors, well over two million yearly, arrive daily by air from points throughout the world via international airlines, from visits to Maui's neighboring islands on one of the state's inter-island airlines, or via one of several stately cruise ships that visit Hawai'i. Inter-island Airways' Sikorsky aircraft introduced air travel to Maui in 1939, and eventually grew to become Hawaiian Airlines.

Throughout its history, its royal wars and its constant economic evolution, Maui has retained its character as a stylish, enchanted playground – first for the Hawaiian *Ali'i*, or royalty, and in recent times for worldwide visitors. Today Maui hosts the world's finest golfers, tennis players, windsurfers, cyclists, equestrians, sailors – and visitors.

There's action and adventure in the surf at Ho'okipa.

The course at Kapalua attracts world-class golfers. 33

Maui has many sights – and many ways to see them.

" Celebrities walk its streets unobtrusively "

A cliff diver prepares for his nightly ritual at Kāʻanapali.

Maui also houses the finest hotels in the world. Celebrities walk its streets unobtrusively, live on its shores, and contribute to its cultural heritage. Today's Maui has a symphony orchestra and local theater groups that bring modern and classic plays to residents and visitors alike. Maui's art community is comprehensive and celebrated worldwide. And the spiritual community continues to seek out the island's solace.

But it is the quiet warmth of Maui's people – their dedication to their island culture and heritage evidenced in every *Mahalo* (Hawaiʻi's "thank you") murmured, or every lyric hula or torch-lighting ceremony performed – that forms Maui's true spirit and appeal.

The history and personality of Upcountry is etched into the face of this Mauian.

The beach at Kā'anapali is a picture of carefree relaxation all year 'round.

The shadows of night paint a hauntingly beautiful portrait of West Maui.

Perhaps providing such a home for peace and play was what the mischievous Māui had in mind all the time.

Amiable, peaceful Maui has become a preferred destination for relaxation-seekers from all walks of life.

It begins with the faintest hint of purples and oranges –
flickers only, at first, flirting with the blackness of early morning.
And then as if in concert with God's own breath, a splendid golden
dawn arrives and the sun rises through the mist – slowly and
dramatically – from the embrace of the rugged crater known
as *Haleakalā*, House of the Sun.

HALEAKALĀ —
DAY BEGINS IN THE HOUSE OF THE SUN

*Haleakalā's spectacular sunrise ignites the sky and dwarfs the crowd
that has gathered to greet the day.*

Warmed by the arrival of a Maui sun.

*" keeps watch
over the antics of the sun "*

The 10,023-foot volcano rises from the island's eastern floor and keeps watch over the antics of the sun. The ancient Hawaiians said the sun lived in the bosom of Haleakalā. The legend lives today – for even with the chill and blackness of early morning, everyone who comes to Maui, including the most ardent late sleepers, seems compelled to witness this most spectacular of natural theatrics.

Haleakalā, the heart of Maui's land mass, is actually less than one million years old as measured by lava rock believed to be from the volcano's initial stages and now evident along the rugged north coast of the island.

The rare Silversword plant enchants visitors of any age.

Haleakalā — House of the Sun.

" home today to many of the island's earliest plant and animal species "

Built in stages beginning with the earliest explosions of lava from the depths of the ocean floor, the crater spewed molten lava, layer upon layer until the mass broke through the waterline, continuing to rise with each additional fiery eruption. Haleakalā's deepest base lies 19,000 feet under the sea, and the last stages of volcanic eruptions created three enormous cinder cones, the largest of which towers nearly one thousand feet above sea level. Its last eruption was in 1790.

Haleakalā is home today to many of the island's earliest plant and animal species, eventually forced into seclusion by new breeds introduced through a continuing stream of immigrants arriving from other areas of the world. For example, the lovely and wistful *'Āhinahina* or Silversword plant which proudly blooms only once and then dies off, grows nowhere else in Hawai'i but on Haleakalā, and is a protected species. Not long ago it neared extinction after the continuous plundering of its rare blossoms.

Science City on the rim of the crater seems a fitting addition to the moon-like landscape of Haleakalā.

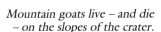
Mountain goats live – and die – on the slopes of the crater.

The Hawaiian state bird, the *Nēnē*, believed to be a descendant of the Canadian goose, also resides in the bosom of Haleakalā. The Nēnē migrated to Hawai'i before the humans, and only a few years ago was nearly extinct. Conservationists' efforts have helped to restore the population along with that of other native Hawaiian birds such as the *'Apapane*, the *'I'iwi* and the *'Amakihi*, who call Haleakalā home.

Hawai'i's state bird, the Nēnē, is one of Haleakalā's most popular residents.

"*resides in the bosom of Haleakalā*"

Although sunrise is the most sought-after view from Haleakalā, sunset brings drama of its own.

" a surprising blanket of snow
also shows up from time to time to greet the sun "

The plant residents of nearby Hosmer Grove have origins in the Himalayas, Japan and Australia, and once grew abundantly in Maui's lower lands.

All of Haleakalā's plant and animal residents live in a stark desert-like terrain. Like other desert areas, the temperatures drop dramatically at night at the higher elevations and it is common to see visitors waiting for the appearance of the sun huddled together, wrapped in layers of sweaters and jackets. An occasional but surprising blanket of snow also shows up from time to time to greet the sun. The ancient Hawaiians told of a battle of wills between Lā, the sun god, and a beautiful snow goddess. No matter how much the sun god evoked the blazing fury of fire goddess Pele, the snow goddess was able to cool the flames with a quiet mantle of white.

Visitors from many countries crowd the observation deck on the crater's rim to watch the beginning of a new Maui day.

Early hikers of the Haleakalā slopes made journal notations about the magnificent views across the clouds to the tips of Mauna Kea and Mauna Loa on the Big Island.

Haleakalā's crucible is 7.5 miles long, 2.5 miles wide with a circumference of 21 miles.

Those with the grit to hike into the crater or ride horseback to its floor attest to an atmosphere reminiscent of the lunar surface. It is no surprise, then, that Science City, a technology research center constructed in 1960, makes its home near the summit. Originally intended to study the sun – and the hydrogen bomb exploded over Johnson Island, eight hundred miles away – Science City today houses a communications station, University of Hawaii observatory, radar installation, and television relay and satellite tracking stations.

" atmosphere reminiscent of the lunar surface "

Bike tours allow visitors to catch the spectacle of the sunrise, and then enjoy a pleasant ride down the winding roadways through the foothills of Haleakalā.

The simplicity of life in early Hawai'i exists today in the cabins within the Haleakalā crater.

" reflections of the sun painting their verge "

The first recorded ascent of Haleakalā took place in 1828 when missionary Rev. William Richards and two associates climbed to the rim. Richards wrote, "The clouds, which hung over the mountains on West Maui …were scattered promiscuously between us and the sea… far below us …while the reflections of the sun painting their verge with varied tints made them appear like enchantment …To complete the grandeur of the scene, Mauna Kea and Mauna Loa lifted their lofty summits…"

It was a panorama shared by generations who have lived or toiled on the slopes of the volcano since the time of the early Polynesians – and by as many as 25,000 yearly visitors who began hiking the trails as early as 1939.

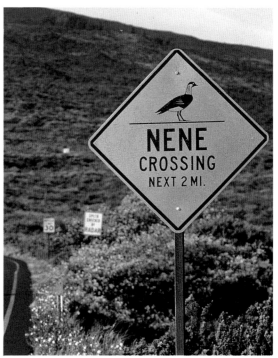

Hawai'i's state bird, the Nēnē, enjoys a unique presence in Upcountry Maui.

Pock-marked in dusty, dramatic mounds, the surface of Haleakalā reminds one of the lunar surface.

Packing into the crater.

" we truly see our own souls! "

Standing deep in the crater, exploring the subtle-hued crystalline surfaces and breathing deeply of the still, crisp air, there is an uncanny feeling of total unison with nature.

No wonder the Hawaiians considered Haleakalā a sacred place. Latter-day explorers, gazing into the crater's crucible through the shimmering multi-hued mists, have seen their own reflection and agreed with the ancients – that through this view, "we truly see our own souls!"

A concert of technology
and nature welcome the sunset.

Taking full advantage of Haleakalā's slopes.

UPCOUNTRY MAUI –
GOLDEN BLOSSOMS ON
THE HILLSIDE

Upcountry Maui, often considered the bread basket of Hawai'i, is a fresco of verdant pastures and colorful ranchlands.

Surely there can be no more charming realm of Maui than that which exists in Upcountry – with its panoramic ocean views and rolling ranches, broadly washed in the most vivid emerald shades and punctuated with patches of floral colors. From the missionaries and whalers to today's Hawai'i ranchers and frequent visitors, Upcountry Maui has been called one of Hawai'i's unique corners.

*" where folks move about today
as freely on horseback as by automobile "*

This is the countryside where proud pheasants strut and mountain goats play host on the upper slopes of Haleakalā, where folks move about today as freely on horseback as by automobile, where gracious ranches sprawl in the sun. It is also where the earliest settlers sought peaceful solace from turbulent journeys across the Pacific, and where Asian immigrants who had fulfilled their contracts to work in the sugar and pineapple fields settled.

Colorful Kula with its fields of flowers.

Tending sheep today isn't much different from yesteryear's herding techniques.

A joyful ride through the Upcountry hillside.

" rekindled the heart, soul and energy of quaint Makawao "

Here in Upcountry Maui are the roots of Hawai'i wrapped gracefully in the arms of contemporary America. Visitors have often likened it to the wide open splendor of Wyoming, graced by Hawai'i's own floral species and rural lifestyle. The followers of the windsurfing community in nearby Pā'ia have steadily migrated upward into Makawao, creating a charming mix of country and contemporary upscale shops and businesses. Capuccino bars and collectibles shops grin from every corner of this lovely town. It is a heartwarming renaissance for Makawao, once a booming sugar mill town, reduced dramatically by the decline of the industry. A growing number of windsurfers from around the world, as well as a growing visitor population, have rekindled the heart, soul and energy of quaint Makawao on the slopes of Haleakalā.

The popularity of Makawao has been helped considerably by the influx of windsurfing fans at nearby Pā'ia and Ho'okipa.

Picking today's protea blossoms.

Further up those slopes, the hills of Kula resemble a flamboyant artist's pallet as expanses of orchids, protea, heliconias, and other exotic as well as traditional flowers dance as far as the eye can see. Palm trees and hibiscus of the sea-level tropics give way to hollyhocks, jacaranda and eucalyptus trees. Today's famous Maui or Kula onions come from the farms of Upcountry Maui – onions so sweet and succulent they have won hands-down competition for best flavor the world over. Even the luscious grapes that are used to make champagne are grown in the rich volcanic soil!

The development of Upcountry Maui into one of the islands' most prolific cornucopias is not surprising. It was here that the ancient Hawaiians planted taro and sweet potatoes – staples of their culture's diet. When the whaling ships arrived at Mā'alaea Harbor, the demand for Irish potatoes instigated a new crop. And to see a ship flying a white flag meant that farmers loaded produce into wagons and headed for the wharf to barter and sell.

" resemble a flamboyant artist's pallet "

The Old Cowpoke at 'Ulupalakua.

Kula's dramatic protea flower has become a symbol of elegant floral design throughout the world.

Inhabitants of the Haleakalā Ranch grace the volcano slopes.

Upcountry goods were traded throughout America from as early as the Civil War when Union soldiers were uniformed in garb made of Kula cotton because materials from the South were no longer available to them.

The relatively short ship's journey to California made trade with this adventurous new territory so convenient that during the California gold rush, Maui peaches, pears, plums, potatoes, wheat and other staples fed the '49ers. The prosperity of this quiet hillside farmland gained it the name *Nu Kaliponi* – or New California.

Taro fields gave way to rice fields as immigrants from Asia discovered Upcountry Maui, and in the mid-1800s, the rice fields gave way to sugar plantations. Miles and miles of waving cane became a trademark of the island. But even that staple was quick to pass in Upcountry Maui

" Nu Kaliponi – or New California"

The congregation of the Holy Ghost Church in Kula is treated to a spectacular view of the coastline.

Pā'ia was once the sugar capital of Maui.

Taro patches are a traditional part of the Upcountry bounty.

In 1856, whaling ship captain James Makee, weary of the violent and stormy life at sea, bought a sugar plantation in Upcountry Maui, constructing a village for the workers and a large home for his family. The spread extended from the top of Haleakalā fanning to the ocean from Kīhei to Mākena Beach. Makee worked the sugar for 27 years and then converted the land into pastures and imported his first herd of cattle. His splendid Rose Ranch became a haven for visiting dignitaries, celebrities and royalty over the years and is known today as the 'Ulupalakua Ranch. It is on these premises that the Tedeschi Vineyards was founded when current ranch owner C. Pardee Erdman and California wine-maker Emil Tedeschi combined talents to create the state's first winery.

Quiet afternoons in Upcountry.

" a haven for visiting dignitaries, celebrities and royalty "

Upcountry's newest crop – grapes for fine wine and champagne.

Tedeschi Vineyards occupies an historic location on the 'Ulupalakua Ranch lands.

Makee's Upcountry ranch neighbors eventually followed his lead, converting their plantation fields into cattle pasturelands. Maui's largest ranch, Haleakalā, surrendered its cane to cattle during World War I after more than four decades of sugar harvesting. Ranching families have since carved out a major presence and a unique personality for the area.

Cattle, horses and the ranch way of life are as much a part of Upcountry Maui as palm trees and sand are of the island shoreline. Both horses and cattle were gifted to King Kamehameha in 1792 and 1803, and subsequently designated a protected species. Cattle roamed unbridled for nearly fifty years and flourished in number until organized ranching emerged. A demand for beef by the whalers created the initial incentive for cattle breeding on the island, and the Reciprocity Treaty of 1876 between the Kingdom of Hawai'i and the United States reinforced the demand with an increase in immigration to the islands, and a loosening of restrictions that made land available to outside ownership.

*" Cattle, horses
and the ranch way of life "*

*Horses are the preferred means of transportation for
some Upcountry folks.*

*Where whaling vessels once signaled Upcountry
farmers to bring their crops to the beach for barter,
ships from many countries and in many shapes,
including the U.S.S. Constitution, now slide
gracefully across the horizon.*

" whopping good times "

Colorful hats are part of the fun at the Rodeo.

Maui's paniolos have proven to be some of the world's most colorful rodeo riders.

A prestigious symbol.

In 1830 Mexican Vaqueros arrived, at the invitation of the King, to help teach the Hawaiians how to ranch, and thereafter Hawaiian "*Paniolos*," or cowboys, became a special breed all their own. With their unique woven hats encircled by colorful floral hat leis, Hawai'i's paniolos learned to ride, rope and herd cattle as well as any cowboy in the famous American West. National rodeo championships attest to that fact, as do the whopping good times evident at the Makawao Rodeo held each year on the Fourth of July. Maui's paniolos have a heritage uniquely their own and are, for the most part, descendants of the early ranch hands. Few other places required the herding techniques that faced the early Maui ranchers. Cattle were driven down the slopes to Mākena beach, then herded – not always willingly – through the surf, tied onto small boats and towed, heads bobbing above the salty waves, to waiting steamers where they were hoisted, animal by animal, on board and taken to market in Honolulu.

Upcountry riders have won world championships, but still enjoy the action at home in Makawao.

71

Saddle sport of a different nature also takes place in Makawao when lightning-quick members of The Maui Polo Club thunder across the field in heated competition. Polo is the legendary sport of royalty, but it began on Maui as a remedy for boredom among the paniolos. Instigated by Haleakalā Ranch manager Louis Von Tempsky one Sunday afternoon, the spirited game soon attracted many prominent islanders – from the Maui gentry, the Baldwins, to O'ahu business-man Walter Dillingham, who introduced polo to the island of O'ahu.

Thundering hooves streak down the playing field in an exhilarating exhibition of polo, the sport of kings – a favorite pastime in Upcountry from the time of the earliest ranchers.

Upcountry friends.

The action becomes intense.

From its bases in Maui and Honolulu's Kap'iolani Park (later moved to the North Shore), polo has attracted European royalty, Hollywood celebrities – and numerous other national figures. General George Patton was an enthusiastic participant while in the islands during the Second World War. The Honolulu and Maui teams have been fierce competitors over the years – from the first match, held in Honolulu after Maui players and their mounts endured a violently stormy channel crossing, played a soggy game and suffered an ultimate defeat!

" General George Patton was an enthusiastic participant "

Fields of orchids in Kula.

" blending together vividly "

Upcountry Maui has indeed developed one of Hawai'i's most unusual personalities. It is a combination of all-American grit, laced with the grace and color of the island's many ethnic cultures – Japanese, Chinese, Filipino, Portuguese – all blending together vividly through the smiles of its ranchers, farmers, craftspeople and sports enthusiasts – all robust in the Upcountry sunshine.

Horses have been an integral part of Maui since George Vancouver introduced them to the King many years ago.

A colt tests his legs.

Working in the carnation fields.

Mākena Beach has long been considered special by nature-lovers on Maui.

Colorful watersports abound off the coast of Wailea.

KĪHEI AND WAILEA — RESORT LIVING IN SUNNY STYLE

The lovely beaches of South Maui are proof positive that Māui's mischievous love of the sun is still at work today. From Kīhei to Wailea to Mākena, these sunny oases are some of the island's favorite contemporary sun spots. Exquisite resorts stretch lazily along the 25-mile stretch of beach, with sparkling golf courses tucked here and there along the hillsides.

Dramatic condominiums gaze quietly to sea along Kīhei's shores, resting at the edge of the Māʻalaea Bay and Boat Harbor. These sun-splashed beaches have become a well-deserved second home for many visitors from around the world. From the first major resort in the area built by early sugar conglomerate Alexander & Baldwin at Wailea, to the most utilitarian condominium, Maui's enchanting atmosphere calls one back again and again.

" one of paradise's most enchanting locations "

And while the shoreline today with its sparkling necklace of impressive condominiums and island-style shopping centers meets all the whims of a contemporary culture, the true essence and spirit of the island has not really changed since the earliest explorers first saw these shores.

In their journals, they wrote of forests of tall trees, of coconut palms and small enclaves of thatched huts along the shoreline. It was, they wrote, one of paradise's most enchanting locations. And, once the news spread, it also became a busy trade area as more and more settlers arrived.

*Luxury homes
are part of the landscape in Wailea today.*

*A spirit of lighthearted fun is in the air, in perfect
harmony with the island's namesake – Magical,
Mischiveous Māui*

" harmonious blend of man and nature "

What a way to spend a day!

The first European to explore Maui's shores, arrived in this southern region. In 1786 Admiral Jean Francois Galaupe, Compte de la Perouse, disembarked his ship and regarded the tropical panorama before him at a place now named after him, La Perouse Bay. When La Perouse arrived, Hawai'i's harmonious blend of man and nature was strikingly evident. Taro fields resided next to fish ponds; koa trees and coconut palms offered shelter and shade for the smiling, unhurried population.

Royalty of those times made its way from village to village by means of a footpath that wound along the coastline from La Perouse Bay. Today, sandal-footed children and adventurous visitors hike into the area or reach it by four-wheel drive and trace the steps of those ancient Ali'i along the remains of "King's Highway," once the primary route from village to village throughout the island. Remains of the early villages provide insight into the past for those with an explorer's heart.

Cattle were once loaded onto barges on this placid shore, then taken to market in Honolulu.

Wailea hotels offer a paradise playground.

La Perouse, himself, ultimately sailed from Maui and disappeared later at sea. But after his arrival on Maui, and by the 1800s, traders and whalers frequented nearby Mākena and Māʻalaea. Today's arid climate is thought to have developed largely because sandalwood traders depleted the forests that shaded the bays.

The brays of cattle eventually became commonplace on Mākena Beach after the establishment of the Rose Ranch, now the ʻUlupalakua Ranch, in upcountry Maui. Herds were driven to market in Honolulu by placing them on barges off Mākena beach.

With the creation of a more amenable means of transporting cattle to market, and over time, Mākena beach has become a haven for peace seekers and nature-lovers.

In the late 1960s and early 1970s, waves of "hippies" found their way to the secluded shoreline. Their tent city prospered and grew until 1972 when it was finally shuttered. A section of Mākena beach, known officially as *Onouli* but nicknamed "Little Beach," retained its reputation and attraction for free spirits with a penchant for sunbathing au naturel.

...ngers aboard this luxury cruise liner are treated to one of Maui's spectacular sunsets.

A lazy afternoon on the azure waters off Kīhei.

*" the most perfect
kind of underwater paradise "*

Oneloa or "Big Beach" stretches beyond an
imposing 360-foot cindercone called Pu'uola'i,
and the nearby 'Āhihi-Kīna'u Natural Area
Reserve boasts of fascinating and unusual
marine life living in close-in tidal pools.

    Off Kīhei is the spectacular marine world of
Molokini, an extinct volcano crater, half of
which has broken away. Living in the graceful
semi-circle is some of Hawai'i's most intriguing
marine life. It is a wonderland for scuba and
snorkel aficionados – as fluorescent yellows and
oranges, brilliant greens and purples flash
through clear azure waters. Coral formations
and undersea vegetation create the most perfect
kind of underwater paradise.

A brilliant and fascinating underwater world exists around Molokini, the extinct volcano crater off the coast of Kīhei.

Snorkel and scuba enthusiasts hasten to Molokini on a sunny day.

The appeal of the South Maui shoreline varies – but it is definitely there – whether it emanates from fascinating underwater exploration, the excitement of snagging the day's first marlin, the satisfaction of a putt well executed on the 18th hole of one of Wailea's challenging golf courses, a gourmet dinner in an elegant hotel, the fragrance of the intoxicating plumerias, the laid-back warmth of Maui's people or merely the glorious feel of the sun on one's face.

No wonder Kīhei beach has become a favorite on Maui.

" a putt well executed on the 18th "

Wailea has gained a reputation as one of the world's loveliest golf courses – for good reason!

A golfer enjoys the well-maintained greens in Wailea.

WEST MAUI SHORES –
A COURTSHIP WITH THE SUN

A special ray of Maui's golden sun shines directly on her western coastline. Nowhere else in the world is there a playground that so richly melds the earth's natural wonders with the modern elements of her society. From Lahaina to Kapalua the coastline twinkles with the stars of resortland – stately high-rise hotels offering the best of Hawai'i's hospitality, whispered secrets of Maui's past in the quaint and ever-traditional town of Lahaina, and the profusion of the playful humpback whales that winter just offshore!

Lahaina's sunny coastline.

Kā'anapali Beach is the playground for sunseekers from all over the world.

The Carthaginian and Pioneer Inn are colorful reminders of Lahaina's vivid whaling days. 93

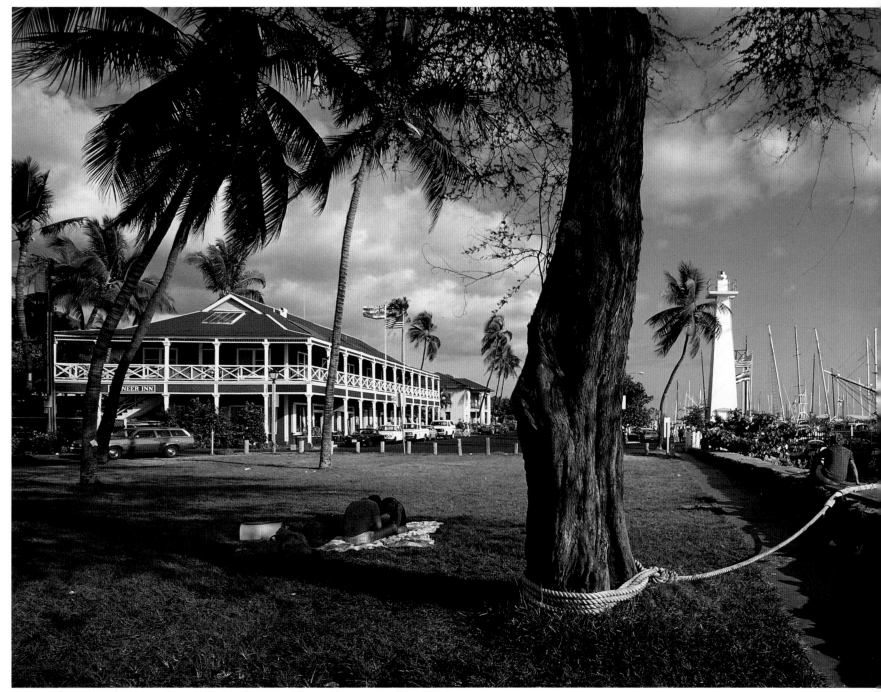

Even on busy days there's a quiet and quaint charm to this popular town on West Maui.

" like no other historic town in Hawai'i "

Contemporary shops are located in the historic buildings that still comprise Lahaina's main street.

Lahaina is like no other historic town in Hawai'i. While city fathers have preserved the classic architecture from the days of the whalers, modern shops have moved into the uneven, wooden buildings that line Lahaina's streets, selling stylish fashions alongside whimsical T-shirts. In the more than 80-year old Pioneer Inn, upstairs rooms are still rented to honeymooners and other guests. Any day of the week tour drivers dressed in their traditional brightly colored aloha shirts gather around scarred tables to "talk story" and wait for their precious cargo of visitors who are perusing the sights of Lahaina town.

The quaint rooms in the historic Pioneer Inn still welcome visitors – just as they did at the turn of the century.

Trendy restaurants serve gourmet dishes, and art galleries intoxicate the senses with aesthetic menus to please every pallet. From art deco sculpture to oil paintings in the fashion of the grand masters, to simple brightly colored posters – nowhere else in America is there such a broad proliferation of art.

But the foundations of this sprightly town are rooted in Hawai'i's past – with yesterday's buildings still the focal point of the town's activity, the endless rhythm of nature its primary attraction, and traditional Hawaiian values the spirit that continuously bids welcome to those who visit – permanently or for just a day.

" intoxicate the senses with aesthetic menus "

A stoic wooden sailor greets visitors to the bar at the Pioneer Inn.

This Hawaiian war canoe replica gives an idea of the type of warfare used by the island kings until Kamehameha united the chieftains and introduced guns into the battles.

Shopping is a popular pastime on the streets of Lāhaina.

" a resortland for the royalty "

Lahaina's reputation as a playground dates back to ancient Hawai'i when, in the early 1700s, King Kamehameha the Great established it as the territory's capital and made it a resortland for the royalty. Even then some of the island's most lavish lū'aus were held on these grounds, capturing the whim of the party-goers – often for days at a time!

Deep-sea fishing off Lahaina's coast attracts thousands of sports enthusiasts each year.

" a sense of spiritual abandon "

Its emergence as a whaling port, long heralded by fable and textbook alike, began in October of 1819 with the first visit of a six-ship Yankee whaling fleet led by the *Balena*. It was a particularly favorable time for these weary seafarers – anxious for respite from their travels and hungry for recreation. No place could have been more accommodating than Lahaina – with its lush tropical shores, its warm fun-loving people – and a sense of spiritual abandon resulting from the tumbling of the traditional religious structure, instigated by Ka'ahumanu, widow of Kamehameha the Great.

Scuba and snorkeling are popular pastimes on Maui.

World-class golf at Kāʻanapali and Kapalua attract top-notch golfers to the area.

The dramatic northwestern coast of Maui has long appealed to visitors – from long before the time of the whalers.

The soft light of evening gives way to sunset for diners aboard one of Lahaina's dinner cruises.

" their crews filling the grog shops and inns "

It was into this spirit of new-found freedom that the whalers sailed. Over the years, when they were not at sea tracking, killing and collecting the valuable products from the giant whales, they contributed their own brand of on-shore revelry to Maui. The reputation of both Lahaina town, and the proliferation of whales in the area, brought more and more whalers. In 1846, 429 vessels were reported to have clogged the harbor, their masts weaving an intricate vertical pattern against the horizon, their crews filling the grog shops and inns of Lahaina. At times as many as 1500 crew members thronged the little coastline village.

The residence of the Bailey family still stands placidly in Lahaina as a reminder of the stature of these missionaries in Maui's history.

Many nationalities and religions are represented on Maui, evidenced by this Jodo Shrine near Lahaina.

*" and life in Lahaina
took on a new dimension "*

In 1823 the missionaries arrived on Maui, and
life in Lahaina took on a new dimension. The
strong presence of this religious faction still
demands attention today through the preserved home of The Reverend Richard Dwight
Baldwin, his wife Charlotte and their eight
children. Although many of the whalers were
in fact of the Quaker religion, many were not.
New laws were passed closing down the grog
shops, establishing curfews and numerous civic
restrictions. The oldest school west of the
Rocky mountains is the Lahainaluna School,
which was opened by the missionaries in 1831.

Kā'anapali Beach provides a picturesque backdrop for weddings.

Dusk settles over quiet and lovely Lāna'i Island, off the coast of Kā'anapali Beach.

Tropical panoramas are typical around Lahaina.

" preferred the free-spirited life of old Lahaina "

Many of the whalers did not easily accept the new ground rules and it was probably no surprise when they rioted in protest. Cannons spit their smoky fire from the casements of the stone courthouse overlooking Lahaina harbor in an attempt to enforce curfews and break up the riots. The basement jail cells of the sturdily-built courthouse were generally filled with characters who preferred the free-spirited life of old Lahaina to that of the new, more refined religious regime.

The whalers were not the only group to find moral conflict with the ways of the missionaries. Lahaina's Luakini Street marks the funeral path of lovely Nahi'ena'ena, sister of King Kamehameha II– both raised in sunny Lahaina. Hawaiian custom allowed brother and sister to marry and bear royal children, but the dogmas of the new American missionaries forbade such interfamilial breeding. The two contradictory beliefs created an irreversible barrier between these two young people, in love since childhood, as the King felt compelled to uphold the laws in the wake of the missionaries' strong community presence. A shattered Nahi'ena'ena died – reportedly of a broken heart – before she reached 22.

The King sent his sister's body home to Lahaina aboard a specially designated ship. Upon reaching the shores of their childhood, the cortege surrounding a simply draped coffin moved along a specially cut roadway, over woven mats, to a mausoleum among tall trees. Long after the death of Nahi'ena'ena, King Kamehameha II found solace by sitting quietly at the grave site of his beloved sister among the kou and breadfruit trees.

Sailors work atop the masts of the historic vessel.

" conflict with the ways of the missionaries "

Her flags flying on a sunny day.

The Carthaginian rests on quiet waters in Lahaina's harbor, a reminder of the exciting whaling days of old.

Sleek yachts now fill the historic Lahaina Harbor.

A hula dancer from a Lahaina tour boat waves the traditional greeting at passers-by.

" the spirit of fun and the soul of the whalers lives on "

Lahaina again experienced a change in its personality with the gradual decline of the whaling industry as American petroleum slowly replaced whale oil in the lamps of fashionable parlors. Then in 1871, the Pacific whaling fleet perished in ice and snow when an early Arctic freeze trapped them in waters off the coast of Alaska. Thus marked the demise of one of Maui's most colorful eras – and the move of Hawai'i's capital to Honolulu in 1843 came as no real surprise.

But the spirit of fun and the soul of the whalers lives on in Lahaina. Ask anyone who has ever visited the Lahaina Yacht Club where hearty sailors of today meet to talk of braving the brisk gusts and currents of the Moloka'i Channel in modern day regattas, or battling the elements from Victoria, B.C. in an annual sailing tournament that is said to test any sailor's command of the winds.

Skeletal remains of whales at the Whaler's Village at Kā'anapali provide a point of interest for visitors.

Sailing enthusiasts find the Maui waters so challenging they have established Lahaina as home base.

The whaling fleets of yesterday have been replaced by whale-watching boats.

Most importantly, there are the thousands of whale watchers who seek a glimpse of Lahaina's gentle giants frolicking in the waters just off the shores. Up to two dozen colorful stalls along the wharf welcome those who want to see this marvel of nature firsthand. From cruises which combine whale-watching with the wonder of other undersea creatures through snorkel excursions, to purely technical voyages out to the playground of the humpbacks, thousands have enjoyed and come to appreciate the play of these ancient creatures.

" gentle giants frolicking in the waters "

Dive boat and rudder fish at Molokini Crater.

A Maui sailor out for a day's adventure.

" *accompany themselves with
soulful songs* "

Moving in "pods," the whales of Maui accompany themselves with soulful "songs," each song established by one dominant leader and joined in by others for up to 18 minutes in length. The "song" changes year to year, with each year's melody pattern evolving continuously from season to season. These ballads, as well as the specific behaviors (i.e. flips, jumps and so on) of the whales have been recorded and studied carefully by scientists. The Cetacean species, including dolphins and porpoises as well as whales, are considered by evolutionists to be an integral part of man's development. The whale songs as well as the chittering conversation shared by dolphins are a form of language not unlike that shared by humans on the earth's dry surfaces.

Each whale movement, such as this familiar tail flip, has been logged and named by Maui biologists.

Dolphin frolicking in Maui waters.

" part and parcel of Lahaina's soul "

The annual visit of the whales has always been part and parcel of Lahaina's soul and spirit. Today's whaling fleet sets its sights on observation and preservation of the humpbacks. Approximately 800 of which migrate here in October each year from Alaskan waters nearly 3,000 miles away, remaining to calve and mate until early spring. Biologists, conservationists and activists such as Greenpeace, the World Wildlife Fund and the Pacific Whale Foundation have long focused on preservation of the whales and through their efforts, the numbers of these gentle giants have increased as more and more nations have ceased commercial whaling.

The Maui-based Pacific Whale Foundation, a non-profit research, education and conservation group, has studied the humpbacks for nearly ten years. Proceeds from their cruises support their continued activities not only in the water off Maui's coast, but as lobbyists in local and national legislative chambers.

An impressive moment of unbounded energy is exhibited by this humpback.

"Freedom in Lahaina" by noted Hawaii scenic artist Anthony Casay.

Whales are not the only creatures at play off Maui's sunny shores.

*" Many world-renowned artists "*

Maui's humpback whales are a particularly precarious breed, monogamous in nature, with a two-year gestation period. Such factors prevent rapid and large increases in herd sizes – and demand even greater attention to preservation. In addition, Hawai'i preservationists are now expanding their focus to encourage man's respect for the natural environment, discouraging interruption of the whale's breeding ground activities by boating enthusiasts and curiosity seekers.

Although nearly two dozen varieties of whales actually visit the Maui waters each year, it is the playful humpbacks that are most visible and most often photographed and painted. Many world-renowned artists have made a home for themselves within the cozy community of Lahaina by painting the whales and their antics in the surrounding waters.

A family of humpback whales.

" *giants bearing
names such as 'Lefty'* "

*Hawai'i's unique Monk seals
are loved and guarded by island residents.*

Often weighing up to 40 tons, Maui's whales
have been "adopted" and named by whale-
lovers through the Pacific Whale Foundation.
Whale supporters throughout the world now
watch yearly for their "wards," giants bearing
names such as "Lefty" (due to a missing left
fin), Humphrey, Ozzie and Spot.

Kāʻanapali's Whaler's Museum offers a graphic history of the whaling era on Maui.

Scrimshaw artifacts include carved objects as well as pictorial scenes.

Maui hosts a large community of scrimshaw artists.

It was through the whalers that the art of scrimshaw became a staple in Hawai'i – and throughout the Pacific. The origin of the word "scrimshaw" is obscured – but some experts say it is derived from the Dutch word "*skrinshander*" or English "*scrinshank*" which both generally mean "idleness." It was during the idle hours aboard the whaling ships that seamen busied themselves by carving on ivory, shell or perhaps a scrap of bone. Most scrimshaw from the early whaling days was carving on whale's tooth, and two types of scrimshaw have since developed. The first is scenic carving on a substance such as ivory, shell or bone. The other refers to the carving of an article – such as a comb, a box or cane.

" scrimshaw became a staple in Hawai'i "

Children enjoy the wildlife at the Hyatt Regency Maui at Kā'anapali.

Kā'anapali Beach attracts beautiful people from all over the world.

Even the large resorts participate in the whaling heritage of Kā'anapali.

" depict the life and time of Lahaina's whalers "

Since the passage of the endangered species law, most contemporary scrimshaw is carved on synthetic or non-animal substances, and is often executed in colored inks. Some of the finest scrimshaw art available today is sold in the quaint shops of Lahaina, ranging in cost from a few dollars for simple souvenir items to many thousands of dollars for elaborate art pieces. Although modern scrimshaw is not always associated with nautical themes, many pieces found in Maui do, quite logically, depict the life and times of Lahaina's whalers.

The whales, of course, are an integral part of the entire life of West Maui – their spouting fountains exploding against the blue horizon just off the sunlit shores of Kā'anapali Beach.

Water sports enthusiasts find plenty of things to do at Kāʻanapali.

" beauty of...our island surroundings"

Today's stately resort corridors are woven with the traditional history and values of the Hawaiians who lived a simple and traditional life on these shores. Even today, along the shoreline from Kāʻanapali up through Kapalua, local fishermen still throw nets to catch an evening's meal.

The staff of the Kāʻanapali Beach Hotel, founded in the mid-1960s, has written its own company mission, stating that "We appreciate the beauty of...our island surroundings and realize that we must preserve it for ourselves and our visitors. We...recognize the need to enhance a sense of place for the mana of the land, its Hawaiian past, present and future..."

Canoe paddling was an ancient sport, but is also a major pastime for local Mauians as well as for visitors.

Windsurfers find challenge in Maui waters.

Not far along the beach, at the Sheraton-Maui, is a volcanic formation jutting out and marking a most sacred Hawaiian place – the point where the souls of the dead are believed to leave earth to become a part of the spirit world. And although the spot is celebrated nightly with a cliff-diving ceremony for hotel visitors, local residents still revere the rock, claiming a continuing existence of departing souls and Hawai'i's famous "night walkers" – warriors trudging the ancient paths of their homeland.

" Hawai'i's famous 'night walkers' "

The undersea adventures available off Kā'anapali are as exciting as those on the water's surface.

The ceremonial night torches are lit at Black Rock Promontory on Kā'anapali Beach.

The glittering necklace of Kā'anapali resorts.

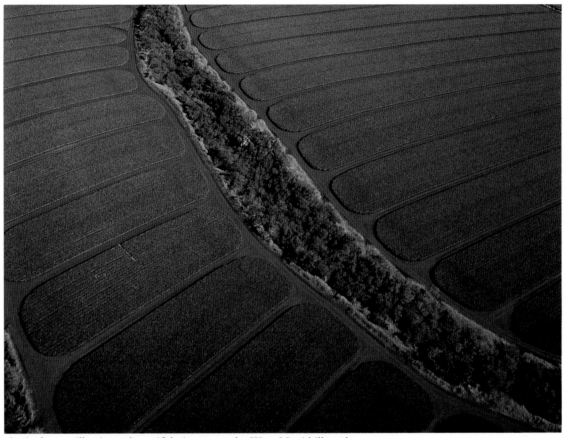

Agriculture still paints a beautiful picture on the West Maui hills today.

As the whalers phased out of Lahaina, a new industry was phasing in adjacent to the Kā'anapali coastline. Fertile soil and an abundance of land inspired entrepreneur off-spring of missionary doctor Dwight Baldwin to begin the cultivation of sugar cane. By 1885 the Pioneer Mill was well into the harvesting of cane, transporting it by means of a small rail-line from Kā'anapali area to Lahaina for shipping.

" a new industry was phasing in "

Lahaina's Pioneer Sugar Mill gives a clue to the previous primary industry on Maui until the tourism industry developed.

Pineapple fields still grow near Lahaina.

Surfing, the sport most often associated with Hawai'i, is alive and well in Maui waters.

The Sugar Cane Train chugs its way along the cane trail near Kāʻanapali, giving tourists a taste of the past.

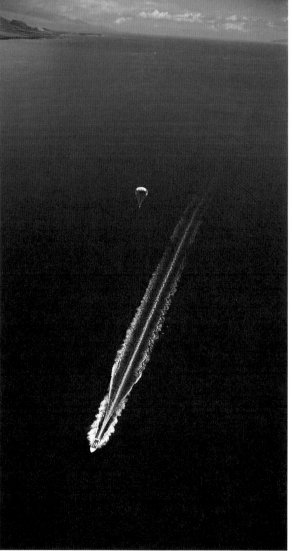

Over time, the mechanization of agricultural systems and truck transportation replaced the field workers and the colorful cane train – until recently when it was restored to carry sightseers along the historic pathway.

" the colorful cane train "

Parasailing offers a thrilling adventure for Lahaina visitors.

Kāʻanapali's verdant golf courses are a pleasure to play.

*" a golden chain
of hotels and condominiums "*

The reign of the tourist in Kāʻanapali was forever established in 1958 when Amfac, a long-time Hawaiʻi corporation, began construction of the three-mile resort complex which now houses a golden chain of hotels and condominiums, as well as the golf courses of Kāʻanapali– considered to be some of the most beautiful in Hawaiʻi. Stretching along the coast to the north through Kapalua are homes, condominiums, the famous Kapalua Golf Course, tennis courts, and breath-taking scenic views which crescendo to a climax at Nākālele – and the cliffs at the northern-most end of the island.

*The colors of the sun
are reflected everywhere at Kāʻanapali.*

137

Kā'anapali resorts are some of the finest in the world.

When the day's activities in the sunshine conclude, there's always lots to do in Maui's resorts.

This is the coastline where the god Māui must have felt his most capricious, for it is here where it seems altogether possible that the mischievous demi-god must have winked at the sun!

THE ISTHMUS AND ĪAO – LINKING THE TWO MAUIS

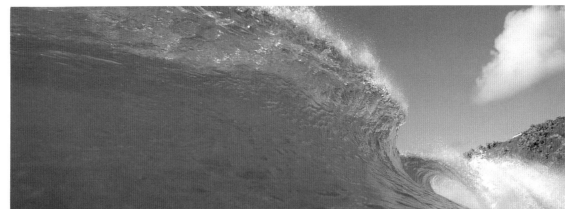

Sparkling surf is available even close to Maui's busy commerce centers in Kahului and Wailuku.

Just as Haleakalā punctuates east Maui with its skyward reaches, the rugged Īao Needle – a 2,250-foot lava spire amid the West Maui Mountains – carves a dramatic exclamation point in west Maui, not far from Kahului. This dramatic spire is situated within the eroded rim of the ancient Puʻu Kukui volcano crater – and is surrounded by one of the lushest, most verdant valleys on the island. In the shadow of the spire is Maui's major business and commerce center, residing in the island's central section and on the narrow isthmus, created by the lava flows from the two major volcanoes now connecting east and west Maui.

Hiking the Īao Valley and its surrounding peaks offers
some spectacular vistas.

The sunny look of Hawai'i always brings a smile.

" land of mirages "

This is the connecting land that the ancient Hawaiians called Kulaʻokaʻaʻmao, "the land of mirages." Kahului, home of Maui's Kahului Airport and its major deep-draft harbor, is only three miles from Wailuku, the seat of Maui's government. The foundation of Maui's sugar cane industry began in this central valley between volcanoes.

Wailuku, a rambling hillside community, is the gateway to the imposing, mist-enshrouded West Maui Mountain range and the treasured Īao Valley cradled in its bosom.

In this dramatic valley, once called the "Yosemite of the Pacific" by Mark Twain, and known by legend as "The Valley of the Kings," emerald-cloaked cliffs gash the earth, dropping into shadowed crevices and then rising again into a mist-enshrouded sky. Crystal streams tumble through the lower elevations and gemlike pebbles tumble through the current. Lush orchids, ferns and ti plants are serenaded by the delicate and melodic songs of the resident bird population, making these slopes and valleys a paradise for the hiker and explorer. From the highest peak in the Īao Valley, spectacular views of Kahului and the surrounding area provide a breathtaking moment.

A canoe crew paddles diligently
in a vigorous competition.

The Īao Needle carries legends and history.

" a blanket of emerald serenity "

*The flowers of Maui
are evident all over the island.*

Even the commercial centers reside comfortably alongside agricultural fields.

Busy Wailuku and nearby Kahului provide most of the island's shopping.

Languishing elegantly within the Īao Valley State Park is the Kepaniwai Heritage Gardens – a graceful village standing in tribute to the many ethnic cultures represented in Hawai'i. Homes and products of Polynesia, Portugal, China, Japan and Hawai'i's other varied cultures are surrounded by vivid and unusual subtropical flowers and plants. The stillness and lushness of the park were described by one visitor as "a blanket of emerald serenity."

Yet this serenity did not come easily to the Īao Valley. Its rugged walls and crevices provided yet another example of the often bloody evolution of the Hawaiian culture. It was here that Kamehameha the Great first used modern warfare to conquer his enemies – and in this case, to capture the island of Maui.

145

Maui business has a style all its own.

Using cannons captured from the vessel *Fair American* off the Kona Coast, Kamehameha, then king of the island of Hawai'i, and his warriors, battled the troops of Maui's King Kalanikupule. The valiant Maui soldiers defended their homeland at Wailuku for forty-eight hours when, bloodied and exhausted, they retreated into their beloved Īao Valley, attempting to escape up its vertical walls. They were quickly overrun by the thunder and fire of a new kind of war devil – gun-power.

The Wailuku river was said to have run red with the blood of these brave patriots. So clogged with the corpses of the fallen was the waterway, the battle was given the name Kepaniwai, "the damming of the waters." Some fifty years later a sea captain exploring the area logged in his journal, "To judge from the appearance, I should think there was many thousand killed and thrown together in heaps."

Tradition is reflected in the Isthmus homes.

" the damming of the waters "

Maui troops suffered final defeat to Kamehameha in the crevices of the Īao Valley.

" A small fish generally used as bait "

Even before the bloody battle of Īao, legend had established the valley as a place of sadness as Īao, a daughter of the god Māui, suffered a heartloss. Īao fell in love with Puuokamoa, a merman god who was turned into a man when he met her at a pool near her home. In an attempt to sever the relationship between his daughter and the troublesome merman, Māui and a powerful Kahuna entangled Puuokamoa in a net and sentenced him to a fiery death. Volcano goddess Pele intervened on the young merman's behalf, however, and convinced Māui to turn the captive to stone as a permanent reminder that he had defied a sacred law. Legend says that the spire of stone rising high into the Maui mist is Puuokamoa, later called Īao – meaning "A small fish generally used as bait."

Popular potato chips from Maui are prepared here.

Maui young people show off typical Hawaiian fashions.

The lovely Ka'ahumanu Church in Wailuku was built in 1832.

Ho'okipa Beach is a favorite windsurfing spot and only a few minutes from Kahului.

" The placid serenity of the valley is well deserved "

It may be of interest to note that Īao was not Māui's only daughter to succumb to the charms of inappropriate lovers — and lose them by the law of her father, as you will note when you read about Māui's life in Hāna.

Today the imposing thrust of the Īao Needle stands as a dramatic reminder of all the turbulent history and legend of this area. The placid serenity of the valley is well deserved.

Everyone finds Maui's water sports to be appealing.

Burning off the cane fields near Spreckelsville.

" the seat of the earliest mission work "

In case of fire...

Only a few miles east, Kahului sits as the busy commerce center of Maui –
site of the Kahului Airport which greets millions of visitors yearly from all
over the world, and contemporary shopping malls that provide the major
products and services for the residents of Maui. A deep draft harbor berths
the ocean-going freighters and cruise ships, and was the seat of the earliest
mission work as well. Hale Hō'ike'iki was the home built by the Reverend
Jonathan Green in 1832 on land gifted to the missionary cause by the King
and Maui Governor Hoapili – who held a strong belief that his constituents
should have the ability to read and write. Ten years later the home was
occupied by Edward Bailey, doctor, missionary, architect and scientist, and
an early visionary in the Maui community.

Quiet Maui day.

Working the sugar cane in Kahului.

Two Chinese merchants established the Hung Tai Sugar Works in 1828, Maui's first sugar mill — processing cane that grew wild. By 1863 major acreage was devoted to the planting of sugar, and the Wailuku Sugar Company was established with Edward Bailey as its first manager.

Not far from Kahului en route to the seaside village of Pā'ia are the remnants of Spreckelsville — named for Claus Spreckels, Maui's first sugar baron, a California financier/sugar refiner who came to the island to take advantage of a Reciprocity Treaty with Hawaii King David Kalākaua. The treaty provided duty-free admission of sugar and other products into the U.S.

Spreckels developed the Hawaii Commercial and Sugar Company, the predecessor to today's C&H Sugar Company, constructing one of the most efficient mills to operate in the world, and creating the Hai'kū Ditch, the largest privately owned irrigation system in the country. By 1886 Spreckels had established his own railway to haul cane to Kahului Harbor and into the holds of his own steamships. In 1899, through a series of financial dealings, the Hawaii Commercial and Sugar Company became part of a new financial entity known as Alexander & Baldwin. But not before Spreckels, who was considered an interloper by many local Maui residents, had sailed from the islands in 1898.

The family store is a tradition in Hawai'i.

" one of the most efficient mills to operate in the world "

Even the rare Hawaiian stilt, living in Kanahā pond, finds the sports enthusiasts at nearby Kanahā State Park to be a colorful crowd.

Kanahā Beach is only a few minutes from the airport at Kahului.

Today, with jets taking off and arriving every few minutes at Kahului, and the nearby harbor activity, with the busy and heated government center in Wailuku, Maui's central isthmus still boasts spectacular natural views from serene beaches. The Kanahā Pond, literally within walking distance from the Kahului Airport, was once a royal fishpond and is now a wildlife refuge where the migratory Hawaiian stilt, the heron and gallinule live peacefully. Kanahā State Park provides a dramatic windsurfing and recreational site.

Such contrasts are common on Maui – nature and history residing side-by-side, comfortably snuggled into the embrace of business and commerce – all warmed by the Maui sun.

" nature and history residing side-by-side "

HĀNA – MAUI OF OLD, ALIVE AND WELL

Magical Māui visited the Hāna Coast and was so overwhelmed with its beauty that he settled in with his wife on a verdant hill. One day, gazing out to sea, the powerful god watched as a gentle mist flirted with the sun. Soon a brilliant profusion of colors was reflected from the drops in the mist clouds.

When Māui's daughter was born soon afterward, he named her *Noenoe Ua Kea O Hāna* – "Misty, Light Rains of Hāna."

The Hāna coastline is one of the island's most beautiful sights.

A Polynesian child in her Sunday clothes.

159

Hāna's historic Wānanalua Church.

Hāna's beaches are pristine and secluded.

" sigh of the sea meeting the shoreline "

The child grew into a beautiful young woman and like her father, she loved the shores of Hāna. During her wandering one day she encountered and soon fell in love with a handsome young man named Ka'uiki. Her paramour, however, was the son of the Menehune – Hawai'i's mythical tribe of elves. Māui's discovery of the romance infuriated him and he forbade it to continue. Ka'uiki, he said, was a man of the sea – and was therefore destined to return to it, leaving Noenoe alone. The pain of his daughter's suffering however, convinced Māui to use his powers to help the doomed lovers. He turned the bold young Ka'uiki into a rugged hill, planted close to the spot where Māui himself had first discovered Hāna's enchantment. He then turned his beloved daughter Noenoe into the quiet mists that have ever since caressed the slopes of Ka'uiki.

The legend tells us that the sigh of the sea meeting the shoreline in Hāna occurs when the sea tells the story of the lovers.

Hāna is more a state of mind than a town.

" create a perfect paradise "

Exploring Hāna is a special experience.

Hāna has been called heavenly by generations of Hawaiians since its shores first welcomed the migrating Polynesians. It was in Hāna that the last of Maui's great chieftains, Kahekili, unified his own island by driving out warriors from the Big Island in 1780, from a fortress located adjacent to today's Hotel Hāna Maui.

Isolated from the rest of the island by rugged cliffs and a road that strikes caution into the heart of even the most intrepid sojourner, Hāna today remains one of the most perfect vignettes of how contemporary Hawai'i can and has melded with traditional Hawai'i to create a tropical paradise.

Hāna's coast is often as rugged as it is beautiful.

A Hāna lei stand.

The last of the Seven Sacred Pools.

" of the exhilarating, windswept waters "

Windsurfers at Ho'okipa – just before the road to Hāna begins.

One can reach Hāna by boat, by air, and over the 52 miles of meandering roadway from Pā'ia – a roadway that has become a legend since its construction in 1927. The experience of the legend begins as one leaves the quaint confines of Pā'ia town – once the primary center of sugar commerce. Today its wooden buildings have been painted in colorful facades and house boutiques and sporting goods outlets. The proximity of the exhilarating, windswept waters of Ho'okipa Beach has made Pā'ia one of the top windsurfing capitals in the world.

Once out of Pā'ia, and with an estimated 600 curves, the Hāna road often narrows to a single lane as it crosses over the 54 rustic bridges originally built to accommodate the route. The fact that it has not been converted into a super highway was the decision, indeed the demand, of local residents anxious to preserve their serene home. The road received its first paving in only 1969. Despite curves, narrows and potholes, the Hāna road still offers one of the most exhilarating experiences available to Maui visitors.

Waterfalls tumble from the cliffs that skirt the roadway, and cool, crystal pools nestled into fern-enshrouded grottos such as Puo'o'kamoa are a welcome respite for drivers. Scenic panoramas such as Pua'aka'a State Park and the Ke'anae Valley Lookout provide enough Hawai'i to last most visitors a lifetime. One moment the road is lined by stately Norfolk pines, another it passes under the curved arbors of flower-bearing trees, and at times thick guava trees drip their fruits onto the pavement.

Pineapple fields are still part of Maui's horizon.

Secluded pools offer the Hāna explorer a lovely way to cool off.

" and cool, crystal pools nestled into fern-enshrouded grottos "

*" and taro fields
covered the hillside slopes "*

When the road reaches Ke'anae Peninsula, the official Hāna region begins – an area that has been continuously inhabited since the arrival of the Polynesian settlers – some records say by as many as 75,000 residents. The emerald Ke'anae Peninsula was once covered with fishponds, and taro fields covered the hillside slopes. About the turn of the century, Chinese laborers whose contracts to work the sugar fields had expired converted the fishponds into rice paddies and later into taro patches. This traditional staple of the islands is still the major crop of the peninsula and its symmetrical fields are a welcome sight to travellers along the road.

The tiny Ke'anae School, one of Hawai'i's smallest, has nonetheless boasted a *Kupuna* – a teacher of ancient chants and folklore – for nearly two decades. But such consistency is the legacy of this magical Hawaiian place, Hāna.

Hāna panorama.

Planting taro in a field along the Hāna road.

Macadamia nut plantations have grown up in Hāna today.

" *is as much a mood as it is a location* "

Hāna itself is as much a mood as it is a location – a mood which everyone who lives here celebrates. The gentle slopes of eastern Haleakalā swoop through green meadows and thick eucalyptus and kiawe trees to rugged cliffs and an intrepid sea. Along the way, groves of guava and papaya and bananas shelter tiny, simple homes, as well as the more lavish residences of celebrities who have chosen to call this quiet, obscure heaven home. Those who live in Hāna will tell you they treasure its discretion.

A church placidly resides in Keana.

A good mud fight among the taro patches in Hāna.

The original symbol of today's Hāna Ranch and hotel.

One of the many single-lane bridges along the Hāna road.

Stopping to explore a waterfall en route to Hāna.   173

Aviator Charles Lindbergh was buried on the grounds of the Palapala Ho'omau Church in Kipahulu near Hāna.

Charles Lindbergh's grave-site.

It was this discretion that brought famed aviator Charles A. Lindbergh and his wife Anne here in 1968. Purchasing five glorious acres overlooking the water from his old friend Pan American Airways Vice President Samuel Pryor, Lindbergh spent his last few years in Hāna. Diagnosed with cancer, he returned to his cottage on the seacliffs and died there only a short while later. This international hero was laid to rest under the mango trees in a simply marked grave which he himself designed, by a cortege of local friends including his nurse, the owner of the local service station, and a policeman.

The grave site at the Ho'omau Congregational Church in Ki'pahulu is visited today by thousands of visitors. In fact, more than 300,000 automobiles annually make the trek through Hāna to the sparkling seven pools, just a few miles before Kipahulu.

" laid to rest under the mango trees in a simply marked grave "

" a giant lava rock cross …
looking across the grazing lands
… and out to sea "

Gannets enjoy the sunshine off the coast of Hāna.

Services are still held in this historic Hāna church.

Throughout most of its history, Hāna has been one of the country's few "company towns," owned almost entirely by the Hāna Ranch. The town consists of a sprawling hotel, a restaurant, market, post office and bank. With the multi-million dollar upgrading of the hotel in 1986, even more visitors have been attracted to Hāna.

The Hāna Ranch was founded and run by Paul Fagan who, in the 1940's, converted his sugar plantation and a newly acquired 14,000 acres to cattle ranching. This conversion depleted jobs for the Hāna residents and in an effort to restore their self-sufficiency, Fagan opened a small resort. In the ten years to follow, the Hotel Hāna Maui gained a reputation as one of the loveliest resorts anywhere, and in the wake of its popularity, Fagan developed the tiny two-block Hāna Ranch Center. After his death in 1959, a giant lava rock cross was erected on a hillside looking across the grazing lands to the plush grounds of the hotel and out to sea.

Today, cattle are still bred on the slopes above Hāna, but new animal technology has fostered "holistic herding" where the cattle are moved frequently to protect the undergrowth. These days, Hāna sightseers exploring the hillsides by horseback, punctuate the horizon almost as often as do the actual ranch hands.

Cattle on the Hāna Ranch pasturelands.

The best way to see Hāna is in a hearty vehicle that will handle dirt roads and hillsides.

" *Immortalized in song* "

There are a few small bed and breakfast inns in Hāna. Serving them, and the rest of the community, is the intrepid Hasegawa General Store, a landmark along the roadway. There, one can find everything from sunglasses to fishing gear, bakery items to dog food. Immortalized in song – and holding a proud place on every map of Maui – the Hasegawa General Store is also one of the only spots for road-weary travellers to stop a moment and enjoy a cool soft drink.

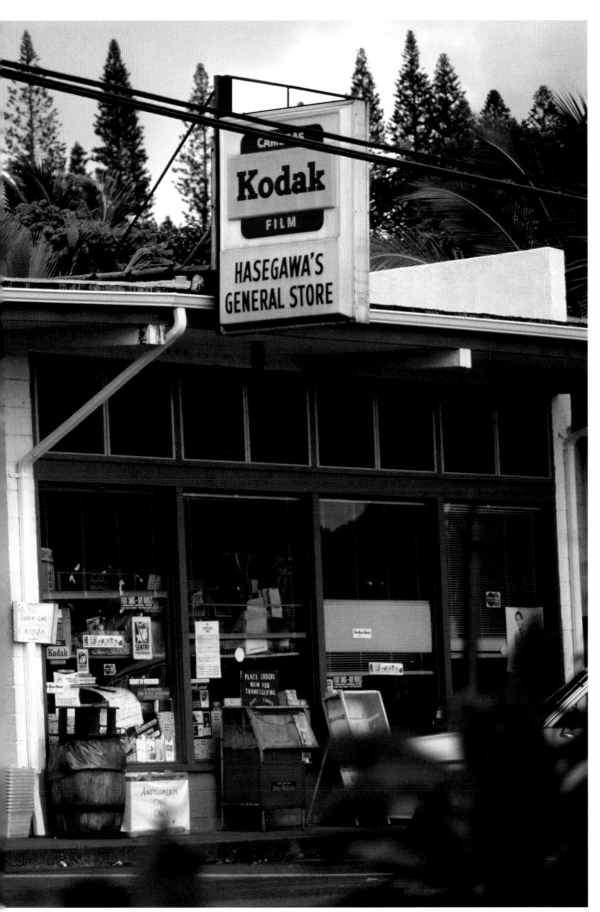

The Hasegawa General Store, Hāna's famed mercantile center.

Hāna is the heartbeat of Hawaiiana tradition.

" lovely, quiet, untouched "

Because of its secluded location, Hāna has remained virtually unchanged over the past decades. Its local residents have worked the same jobs in the hotel, or on the range, or down the road in the taro patches – with a quiet, easy satisfaction. Here in Hāna one finds a large focus on true Hawaiian bloodlines. And it is here that the spirit of the Polynesians is most obviously manifested today.

It is lovely, quiet, untouched, and was intended to remain so. The god Māui left his daughter Noenoe to oversee Hāna, caress its peaks and valleys in the form of a heavenly, rainbowed mist that watches lovingly every day from the sun's own lanai.

Quiet reflections along the shore.

Rainbows are one of Hāna's blessings.

QUIET RECOLLECTIONS
FROM UNDER A MAUI SUN

Magical, mischievous Māui conjured up such riches for his island namesake – and made them possible because of the sun's commitment to shine. So much whimsy, so much romance – from the loving relationship of Hāna's legendary peaks and their caressing mists, to the colorful paniolo legacy in Up-country Maui, to the soulful songs of the whales off Lahaina's coast. Maui may change a little with each passing year – but it never loses sight of its soul. All of us who know Maui recognize that while its essence may lie in its legends, its ancient heritage and its contemporary style, its spirit is all-pervasive.

And to be here – if only for a short while – is truly to catch a glimpse of our own soul.

There cannot be a more exhilarating place on earth to experience that joy than Under a Maui Sun.

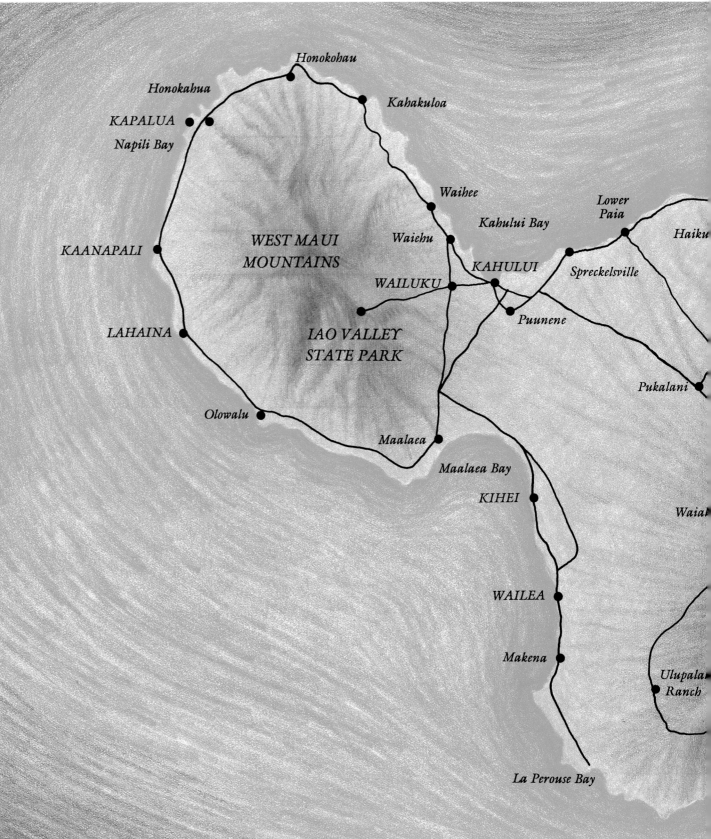

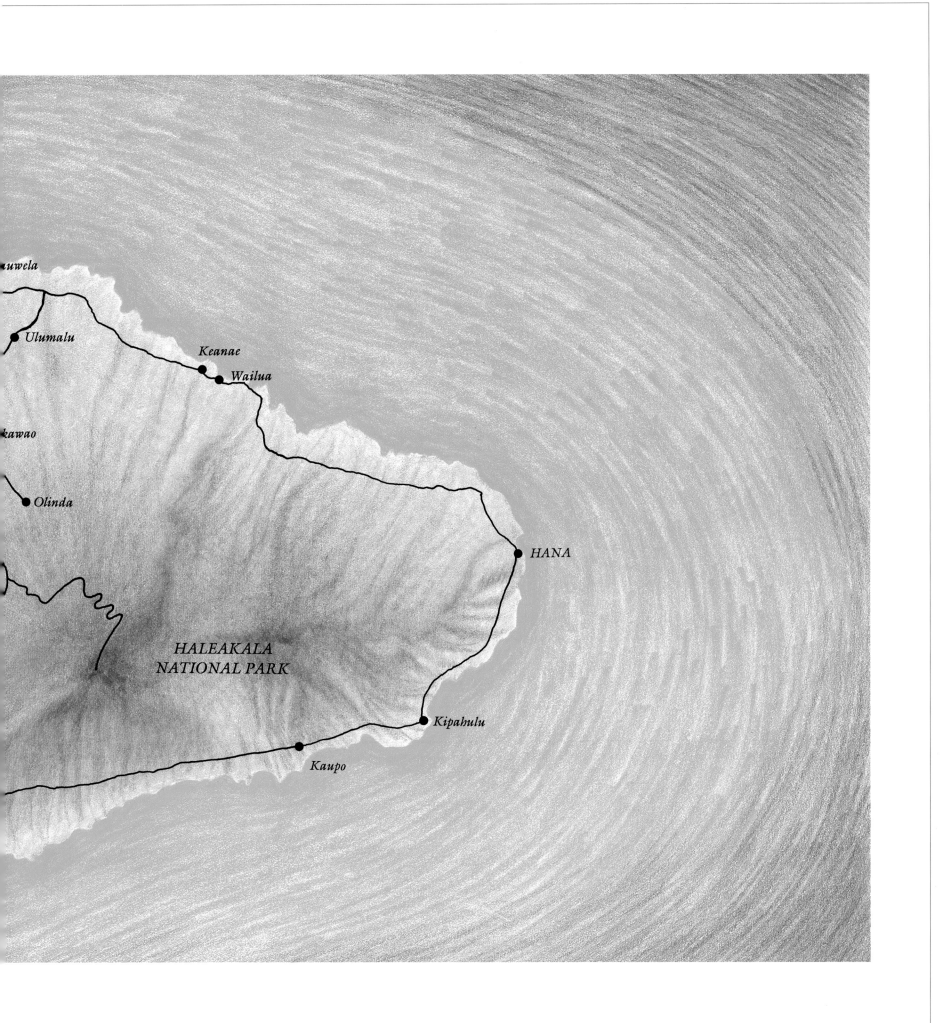

uwela

Ulumalu

Keanae

Wailua

kawao

Olinda

HANA

HALEAKALA
NATIONAL PARK

Kipahulu

Kaupo

ACKNOWLEDGING THOSE
PHOTOGRAPHIC ARTISTS
WHO HAVE CAPTURED
THE SPIRIT AND BEAUTY
OF MAUI

SPECIAL THANKS TO THE FOLLOWING FOR THEIR PHOTOGRAPHIC CONTRIBUTIONS:

Bishop Museum Photographic Archives
Hyatt Regency Maui
Pacific Whale Foundation
Sheraton Hotels
Whalers Village Museum

* Courtesy of Stock Photos Hawaii

BIBLIOGRAPHY

THE ESSENTIAL GUIDE TO MAUI
Scott C.S. Stone
Island Heritage, a Division of the Madden
Corporation, Honolulu, Hawaii
Copyright 1988

GUEST INFORMANT — MAUI
Published by LIN Broadcasting Corporation,
New York
Copyright 1988

KIHEI GOLD COAST NEWS
Various 1988 Issues

LETTERS FROM THE SANDWICH ISLANDS
Edited by Joan Abransom
Island Heritage Limited
Norfolk Island, Australia - 1975

MAUI–The Last Hawaiian Place
Robert Wenkam, Friends of Earth, San Francisco,
New York. Copyright 1970 Friends of Earth
Distributed by McCall Publishing Company,
New York

MAUI GOLD
Winter 1988
Published by Maui Gold Inc.
Copyright 1989

MAUI ISLAND GUIDE
January 1989
Guide Magazine, Honolulu, HI
Copyright 1989

MAUI NO KA OI
Robert Wenkam
Rand McNally and Company, Chicago, 1980

MAUI ON MY MIND
Rita Ariyoshi
Mutual Publishing of Honolulu
Copyright 1985

MOWEE
An Informal History of the Hawaiian Island
Cummins E. Speakman, Jr.
Pueo Press
San Rafael, California
Second Edition 1984
Copyright 1978

ON THE HANA COAST
Ron Youngblood
Emphasis International Ltd. and Carl Lindquist
Second Edition 1987
Copyright 1987

REMARKS ON "THE TOUR AROUND HAWAII"
BY THE MISSIONARIES
E. Sanders for Mssrs. Ellis, Thurston, Bishop and
Goodrich in 1823
Printed for the authors - Salem, 1848

ROAMING IN HAWAII
Harry A. Franck
Frederish A. Stokes Co.
New York, N.Y., 1937

SOUNDINGS
Pacific Whale Foundation
Vol. 3, No. 2. Winter 1988
Pacific Whale Foundation, Kihei, Maui, HI
Copyright 1988

WHALE SONG
A Pictorial History of Whaling and Hawai'i
MacKinnon Simpson and Robert B. Goodman
Beyond Words Publishing Company
Honolulu, Hawaii - 1986

INDEX